P9-APD-157

DRUG USE AND DRUG ABUSE

DRUG USE AND DRUG ABUSE

BY GERALDINE WOODS

FRANKLIN WATTS
NEW YORK ■ LONDON ■ TORONTO ■ 1979
A FIRST BOOK

Photographs courtesy of: the Drug Enforcement Administration: facing p. 1, pp. 6, 10, 26–27, 31, 32, 36 right, 41, 44; Photo Researchers, Inc.: pp. 16 (Rapho/© Paul Sequeira), 21, 36 left (Carl Frank); Religious News Service: pp. 22 left (United Press International), 22 right (Don Rutledge); Argonne National Laboratory: p. 51; United Press International: p. 52.

Cover design by Beehive Design Studio, Inc.

Library of Congress Cataloging in Publication Data

Woods, Geraldine.
    Drug use and drug abuse.

    (A First book)
    Bibliography: p.
    Includes index.
    SUMMARY: Outlines the medicinal and recreational use of various drugs including narcotics, amphetamines, tobacco, alcohol, and over-the-counter drugs such as aspirin and cough syrups.
    1. Drug abuse—United States—Juvenile literature. 2. Drugs—Juvenile literature. [1. Drugs. 2. Drug abuse] I. Title.
HV5825.W575   615'.1   79–11739
ISBN 0–531–02941–7

CONTENTS

WHAT IS A DRUG?

Turn on your television set. Chances are, in less than an hour you will have seen at least one person trying to sell you a **drug.** Do you have a cough? Try this cough syrup. Is your foot itchy? There is a cream to cure it. Are you sleepy, or unable to sleep? Do you have a headache, an upset stomach, a toothache? There are drugs available that can supposedly take care of all these problems and many more.

Drugs have always been popular, even in the oldest civilizations. The ancient Greeks, for example, would calm their nerves with a soothing tea made from the poppy flower. Several thousand years ago, the Egyptians used castor oil to relieve intestinal ailments. The ancient Romans had a drug that strengthened a weak heartbeat.

In many religions, drugs have been used as part of regular religious ceremonies. **Tobacco** was smoked by the Maya Indians of Mexico as an offering to the gods for rain. The Maya also believed that tobacco could ward off ghosts and evil spirits. Some North American Indians ate a small dried mushroom as part of their religious ceremonies. This mushroom contains a substance called mescaline. Mescaline is a powerful drug that makes the user see strange visions.

Even today, drugs are used in many religious celebrations. For example, wine, which contains the drug **alcohol,** is used in some Christian services and during many Jewish ceremonies.

A drug is a chemical substance that, when taken into the body, alters a person's bodily processes. If a person is sick, certain drugs can help restore the body to normal. **Medicines** for the body and mind are drugs that do this. Many substances used for recreation, such as alcohol and tobacco, are also drugs. These are drugs that cause the body to function differently than normal.

DRUGS USED FOR THE TREATMENT OF ILLNESS

When the average person thinks about drugs, the first thing that comes to mind is sickness. This is because one of the most important uses of drugs is in the treatment of illness.

Some drugs can actually cure a disease. **Antibiotics,** for example, are drugs that fight against certain bacteria germs. Bacteria can cause many serious illnesses such as scarlet fever, whooping cough, and tetanus. Some antibiotics kill the germs. Others only weaken them enough to enable the body to heal itself.

Other drugs only help sick people feel better, without actually curing their illness. These drugs treat the symptoms, or signs of the disease. Someone who has a cold, for example, can take drugs to dry up a runny nose or bring down a fever. But there is no drug to cure the cold itself. In most cases, though, the cold will soon disappear without any help from drugs.

Still other drugs are used for sicknesses of the mind. Nearly all of us experience at least some emotional discomfort every day of our lives. A disappointing grade on a test or a fight with a parent can cause hurt feelings. And most people have to deal with serious emotional distress at some time in their lives, perhaps when someone they love dies. These sensations are not physical, but they are painful just the same.

Most of the time people face their emotional troubles without help from doctors or medicines. A long talk with a friend, a movie, or even a good night's sleep is enough to get them through. But sometimes this is not enough. A person may stay nervous or unhappy for long periods of time, be unable to work, study, or have fun.

There are drugs that help people when they cannot cope with emotional pain. These drugs work on the brain and nervous system of the body and change the way we feel. People feeling very nervous, for example, might take a drug that helps them to feel more relaxed. People whose problems keep them awake at night might take a drug that helps them to sleep. None of these drugs, however, can remove the underlying problem that led to the emotional upset in the first place.

Prescription and Over-the-Counter Drugs
Because expert knowledge is needed to use them safely, the most powerful drugs used in the treatment of illness are strictly controlled. They can be bought only if they are ordered, or prescribed, by a doctor. This type of drug is called a **prescription drug.** The written order the doctor writes for the drug is called a prescription.

When you need a powerful drug, a doctor will prescribe it for you. The doctor will also give you careful instructions on how to use it. This information will appear on the container you get from the pharmacy.

Less powerful medicines, such as nasal sprays, aspirin, and some cough syrups, can be bought by anyone. These medicines are usually called **over-the-counter (OTC) drugs,** because they can be bought by simply giving money "over the counter." People don't need a doctor's prescription to buy OTC drugs.

However, just because these drugs do not require a prescription does not mean they are harmless. Not at all. They are simply *less* likely to cause harm if misused. NO DRUG IS SAFE IF IT IS TAKEN CARELESSLY. To help you choose and use OTC drugs wisely, manufacturers nearly always supply printed labels with information on what the drug is for, who can take it safely, and how to take it safely. If you are unsure about a particular item, ask your druggist.

DRUGS FOR RECREATION

Since drugs change the way we feel not only physically but psychologically too, many people take drugs to change their mood. Drugs are an important part of most social events. People invite friends for "a cup of coffee" or "some nice hot tea." Coffee and tea both contain small amounts of the drug **caffeine.** At many parties one or more forms of alcohol are served, such as beer, wine, or whiskey.

Drugs are also taken by people who are looking for new experiences. These people take drugs out of curiosity, to see what effects these drugs will have on their minds. Other people take certain drugs to lift their spirits, to "get high."

Most of the drugs taken for recreation are described in this book. None have label information for their safe use. Only cigarettes carry any kind of warning at all. This does not mean that these drugs cannot be abused. Many of them are, in fact, quite dangerous and may have powerful and lasting effects on the body. Some have been found to be so dangerous, even taken in moderation, that their use for recreation is against the law. Yet illegal drugs are available—from people who sell them illegally on the street or from friends who have already bought them from a drug "pusher."

Each year, Americans alone buy over $10,000,000,000 worth of drugs to treat their aches and pains. They spend an additional $32,000,000,000 on tobacco and alcoholic beverages. How much is spent on illegal drugs is almost impossible to estimate, but must surely number in the billions also.

Americans are not alone in their liking for drugs, either. All over the world, from the largest cities to the smallest villages, drugs can be found.

It is easy to see that using drugs is very much a part of human life. What is not easy to see is the effect of all these drugs on our bodies.

You will probably at some time be urged by your friends to try one or more recreational drugs. If you are thinking about doing so, you need information. This book can help you get it. Read it, and some of the others mentioned, or contact the organizations listed. Be wise; know what it's all about *before* you take drugs.

OTC drugs being manufactured for sale.

USING DRUGS SAFELY: SOME GUIDELINES

Although each drug is different, there are some general rules for using drugs safely. As we said earlier, no drug is completely safe.

Even aspirin, perhaps the most commonly used OTC drug, can be harmful. Some people are sensitive to aspirin and become sick when they take it. Aspirin taken in large amounts can cause nausea, mental confusion, or even death. Also, aspirin taken in combination with certain other drugs is highly dangerous. Each year, the misuse of aspirin—by intentional overdose or by taking it accidentally in harmful combination with another drug—causes more deaths than any other drug.

But just because drugs can sometimes be dangerous is no reason not to ever take them. Used properly, drugs can save the lives of millions of people. They can soothe the sufferings of millions more. The key to using drugs safely is to use them properly.

CHOOSING THE RIGHT DRUGS

In choosing a drug for a patient, a doctor will take several things into consideration. First of all, the drug must have the right effect on the body. Suppose you have an ear infection. The doctor must select a drug that will kill the germs causing the infection. If the drug can't do what it is supposed to, there is no point in taking it.

This may sound like a sensible idea, but many people seem unable to accept it. Doctors often report that their patients with colds or influenzas want to be given antibiotics, because they've heard that antibiotics are powerful drugs. But antibiotics only work against certain bacteria germs. They are useless against diseases caused by other kinds of bacteria or against colds and flus, which are caused by viruses. The patients become upset and distrustful when their doctor says that antibiotics won't cure the illness they have. They demand the doctor give them the drug anyway!

SIDE EFFECTS

Secondly, the doctor has to consider what other effects the drug will have on the body. Drugs are carried by the bloodstream to all parts of the body. A pill taken for an ear infection, for example, will also go to the heart, the liver, and so on. Thus, while the drug goes to work healing your ear, it may also be making you sleepy or nauseous. These other effects a drug has on your body are called **side effects.**

Before most new drugs are sold to the public they are carefully tested by the manufacturer. The results of these tests are examined by government agencies. If the drug is found to be at least somewhat effective and exhibits only minimum potential for harm—dangerous side effects—it will probably be approved for sale.

In spite of careful testing, however, tragedies can occur. The drug thalidomide, for example, was once given to some pregnant women. Later it was shown that the drug had caused serious deformities in the infants of these women.

Sometimes side effects can take a very long time to show. In the 1940s and 1950s a medicine called diethylstilbestrol (DES) was given to pregnant women who were prone to miscarriage (the death of a fetus before birth). We now know that DES greatly increased the risk of cancer in the adult daughters of women who took this drug. In this unfortunate case, the side effects did not appear until twenty years after the drug was taken.

A doctor will usually test to see what a person's blood pressure is before prescribing a drug—and for good reason.

Blood circulates through the body mostly by way of tubes called arteries. As it flows, the blood presses against the artery walls. The amount of pressure exerted varies from person to person and can be tested and measured.

Many people suffer from a condition known as high blood pressure. Aggravation of this condition can result in serious damage to the arteries. A number of drugs make blood pressure rise. This is a very common side effect, in fact, and a highly dangerous one for people who already have high blood pressure. So most doctors test blood pressure before prescribing any drug.

Knowing a person's blood pressure, by the way, is only part of what a doctor must know in order to prevent drug-related mishaps. Most doctors require a complete medical history (a record of illnesses and individual reactions to common drugs) from a patient before prescribing any drug for that patient.

DOSAGE

The doctor also has to decide how much of a drug a person should take. This is called **dosage.** The dosage for every drug is different. Some drugs are given by the cupful. For others, the tiniest drop might be too much. Dosage also depends on a patient's age, sex, and weight. Women and children usually need less because their bodies are smaller. A very fat person might need more.

COMBINATIONS OF DRUGS

Finally, the doctor has to know what other drugs a patient is taking. Many drugs that are safe alone become killers when taken with other drugs. Sleeping pills, for example, cannot be taken safely with alcohol. This is because both these drugs slow down the activity of the nervous system. The situation is even more dangerous than it sounds. When taken together, these drugs actually increase the effect of each other. The combined effects are much greater than the sum of the parts. Some people call this the one-plus-one-equals-fifty effect. To avoid dangerous combinations, no two drugs—including OTC and recreational drugs—should ever be taken together without discussion first with a doctor.

Filling a prescription properly takes experience and careful attention. A mistake could result in serious harm.

ADDICTION

Habits are so much a part of our lives that it is difficult for us to do without them. To understand this fully, try changing a few of your own habits. If you usually have a light breakfast, fix yourself a big meal. Go to school by a different route. Stay in when you usually go out, and change your bedtime routine. At the end of a few days, you'll probably feel completely miserable. You'll look forward to "getting back to normal." In other words, you'll probably want your old habits back, because they make you feel normal.

Many people who have drug habits tell us that this is why they need drugs—to feel normal. They have taken a certain drug so many times that it has become a necessary part of their lives. Without the drug, they feel uncomfortable and upset.

DRUG HABITS OF THE MIND

Any drug can be psychologically habit-forming, if the person taking the drug believes that he or she cannot do without it. A good example of this is over-the-counter sleeping pills. Scientists tell us that the drugs these pills contain are not really strong enough to cause sleep. Yet many people think they are, and they take them every night before they go to bed. They fall asleep, believing the pill was responsible. Then, if they skip a night, they lie awake, tossing and turning. Since they believed it was the pill that made them sleep, they could not sleep without it.

Sometimes psychological drug habits become very strong. The person's desire for the drug goes completely out of control. The body appears not to need the drug at all. But in the user's mind there is a basic, deeply felt need for the drug. In this case the person is said to be psychologically dependent on the drug.

DRUG HABITS OF THE BODY

Drugs can also be physically habit-forming. After using certain drugs over and over again, the body changes. The drug actually becomes part of the body's chemical makeup. Without the drug, the body will not feel normal. **Amphetamines** are a good example of this. The first few times a person takes an amphetamine drug, he or she is unable to sleep. But after repeated doses, the person begins to sleep normally again. In fact, the regular amphetamine user may find it difficult to sleep if the drug is withdrawn.

The sleeplessness that a regular amphetamine user feels when the drug is not taken is an example of a **withdrawal symptom.** Withdrawal symptoms are unpleasant sensations that occur when a drug the body has grown accustomed to is withdrawn. They vary from drug to drug and from user to user but often include headaches, dizziness, nausea, nervousness, and seizures.

Withdrawal symptoms may be partly psychological. Studies have shown that people who get professional help when they withdraw from drugs tend to suffer less than those who go it alone.

Another sign of the body's adaption to a drug is **tolerance.** Since the body has made the drug part of its regular chemistry, the amount of the drug needed at first may not be enough after the person has been taking it for a while.

If a person uses a calming drug for a long time, for example, his or her nerve cells will change. They will become more excitable, perhaps in preparation for the calming influence to come. A regular user of this type of drug gradually becomes more and more nervous and a larger dose of the drug will be needed to produce a peaceful feeling.

People who develop tolerance to one drug often find they have developed it to other drugs that have similar effects on the body. A person who has developed tolerance to alcohol, for example, may also have tolerance to other drugs that slow down, or depress, the nervous system.

Because a person has developed tolerance to a particular drug does not mean it is then perfectly safe to continue taking it. Repeated large doses of almost all the drugs discussed in this book can do serious damage to body organs.

When a drug habit causes withdrawal symptoms and tolerance, it is usually called **addiction.** In examining or treating an addiction, it is often impossible to distinguish between physical and psychological addiction. A person who has become addicted has become dependent on the drug, in most cases both in mind and body.

CAUSES OF ADDICTION

Scientists do not really understand much about the causes of addiction. Some drugs, such as **narcotics,** usually lead to addiction if they are taken regularly. But a small number of people can take these same drugs from time to time without becoming addicted. Other drugs are addictive only if they are taken over a long period of time.

Some researchers think that all addictions may have a physical cause. Substances called endorphins are produced in the brain. Endorphins are natural pain relievers. People who become addicted to narcotics may not be producing enough endorphins in their own bodies.

Another line of research has shown that the tendency to become addicted to a drug could be inherited. Studies have shown that children whose natural parents were addicted to alcohol are six times more likely to become addicted themselves. This is true even if the children were raised by nonaddicted stepparents.

Studies have shown that a person's chances for addiction may also be affected by the society in which he or she lives. The United States, for example, has a high rate of alcohol addiction. Greece and Italy, in contrast, have a very low rate of alcohol addiction even though drinking in these countries is widespread.

However, most researchers still believe that addiction is at least partly psychological. Addicts often come from broken or unloving families. They tend to have a low opinion of themselves and great difficulty in forming friendships. They also seem to have a greater than normal need for variety and excitement. And finally, most addicts are people who find it particularly hard to

A drug abuse treatment facility in Illinois.

cope with frustration. The addiction becomes a learned way of reacting to frustration.

Suppose, for example, a problem comes up that the person cannot readily solve. Somehow that person gets the idea to escape from it by taking drugs. Perhaps he or she has heard about drugs from a friend. The drugs help the crisis period pass. They make the person feel relaxed or good in spite of the problem. Of course, the problem does not go away, and, even more importantly, the person does not get the chance to improve his or her skill in problem solving, a skill so very necessary to a happy and successful life. As time goes on, the person turns more and more to drugs to cope with life. The unsolved problems pile up and help push the drug user into becoming a drug addict.

In spite of all we've said, there is really no such thing as a "typical" drug addict. People take drugs for a variety of reasons, and addicts can be found in every age group and at every level of society.

TREATMENT OF ADDICTION

Many addicts enter a hospital or drug treatment clinic. There, the dosage of the drug is cut down little by little, or the drug is taken away completely. Other drugs may be given that will relieve the nausea, sweating, headaches, and other physical symptoms of withdrawal.

Psychological help is also usually given at the same time. The best approach seems to be to attack the problems that led the person to drugs in the first place. There are a number of groups that are well known for the psychological help they give, including Synanon, Odyssey House, and Alcoholics Anonymous. In these groups, ex-addicts try to help each other stay away from drugs. Members are taught to depend on each other for support and encouragement, especially when they are tempted to turn to drugs again. Group discussions help bring out the problems that may have led to the addiction.

Another type of treatment involves the use of a substitute drug. This treatment is often used for heroin addiction. The heroin addict receives frequent doses of methadone or LAAM, a newer drug. These drugs seem to satisfy the addict's desire for heroin yet do not produce the drastic psychological and physical changes heroin does. The addict can go to school, hold a job, live a normal life—as long as the substitute drug is being taken. If it is ever stopped, even years later, the addict may desire heroin again.

In still another form of treatment, drugs are given that make taking the addictive drug very unpleasant. A person addicted to alcohol, for example, may be given a drug called antabuse. After taking antabuse, even a small amount of alcohol will make the drinker feel sick.

NARCOTICS

Narcotics were probably among the very first drugs used as medicines. Narcotics are drugs that relieve physical and emotional pain. They also produce sleep or a dreamlike, half-awake state. Most narcotics are made from the poppy flower, but a few are produced artificially in laboratories. Opium, morphine, and heroin are some common narcotics. Morphine is used medically for relief of severe pain. A liquid containing the narcotic codeine is used to quiet coughs. Heroin currently has no approved medical uses, although it has been used experimentally to ease the suffering of patients who are dying of cancer.

Because they are so effective in stopping pain, narcotics could have been some of the most useful drugs we have. Unfortunately, they are some of the most dangerous. This is because all narcotics tend to cause severe addiction. Using these drugs for even just a short time is enough to "hook" most people. And the power of narcotics addiction is such that most people remain addicted for the rest of their lives.

Because they are so addictive, all narcotics are illegal except as prescription drugs. (Heroin is not legal even for medical use yet.) To be sure they are used properly, narcotics are subject to strict government regulation. No amount of regulation, however, has ever been enough to stop the nonmedical use of these drugs. Even though it is against the law, many people buy and take narcotics, especially heroin, without a doctor's prescription. People with emotional problems often use these drugs as a temporary escape from reality. They like the dreamlike state narcotics create. Most people who use heroin, also called junk, for nonmedical purposes become addicted "junkies." As they struggle to supply their habit, their lives become nightmares of searching for, buying, and taking drugs.

Because heroin is the most widely used of the narcotic drugs, we will give it a closer look.

HOW HEROIN AFFECTS THE BODY

Heroin is a white powder that looks something like sugar. It can be inhaled, or dissolved in water and injected into a muscle or vein. Heroin acts mainly on the nervous system of the body, although it affects other organs as well.

When a person takes heroin, the pupils of the eyes become smaller and the rate of breathing is slowed. Most users become constipated and some feel nauseous, short of breath, dizzy, or sleepy.

If these were the only effects, very few people would take heroin. The physical symptoms tell only part of the story. The most important effect of heroin is how it makes people feel emotionally.

Opium growing wild in northern Thailand.

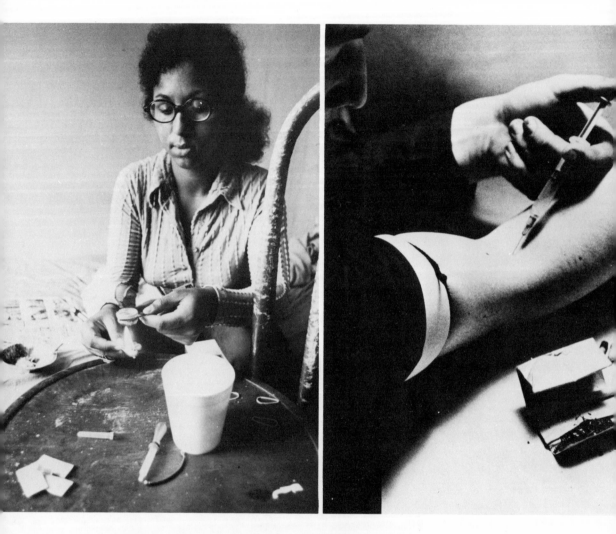

Here a heroin addict is "cooking" her
heroin powder in a bottle cap. The powder will melt into a liquid, be put into
a syringe, and then injected into a vein.

Addicts say that immediately after taking the drug there is a "rush"—a brief period of very intense good feeling—followed by a few hours of complete calm. Some people go to sleep, others remain in a half-awake state. Nothing bothers a person during this stage.

However, only three or four hours after they take the drug, most addicts begin to feel the first symptoms of withdrawal. They become anxious and restless, and begin to worry about finding their next dose of the drug. If in the next few hours they don't get another dose, they will begin to feel physical withdrawal symptoms. These include sweating, aches in the back and legs, a runny nose, chills, fever, nausea, and diarrhea. After three days the worst is over, but weakness, restlessness, and sleeplessness can continue for weeks. Psychological withdrawal takes much longer. A strong desire for heroin has been reported by addicts years after their last dose. Most addicts are unable to stay away from the drug permanently.

OTHER EFFECTS OF HEROIN ADDICTION

The long-term physical effects of heroin addiction are quite serious. Addicts often have illnesses that go untreated because heroin has masked the pain. Their veins collapse from having been injected too often. Their skin, full of needle marks, may be covered with sores. Dirty needles often cause serious infections. Because addicts buy their drugs on the street, they cannot be sure of the drug's purity. Cheaper substances are often mixed with the heroin, so the seller can make a larger profit. Sometimes people die from reactions to these substances. Since they don't know how strong a certain batch of the drug is, many addicts die from overdoses. An overdose of heroin causes the lungs to stop functioning.

The person then dies from lack of air. All of these dangers make the life of an addict a risky one. The death rate for narcotics addicts is twice as high as the death rate for nonaddicts of the same age.

The addict also lives outside the law. Possessing the drug is a crime. And heroin is quite expensive. Addicts must often steal to get enough money to pay for their drugs. Much of the addict's life is spent finding money for drugs and buying a day's supply. Addicts become cut off from everything most people find enjoyable in life. Heroin can really become an addict's whole life.

COMMON NARCOTICS

Name	Description	How Used
Opium	Dried sap of the poppy flower. Causes sleep or dreamlike state. Pain reliever.	Smoked or eaten.
Morphine	An ingredient of opium. About ten times as strong as opium. Used medically as a pain reliever.	Eaten when used for recreation. Injected for medical use.

Name	Description	How Used
Codeine	Another ingredient of opium. Not as strong as morphine. Used in prescription cough medicines and as a pain reliever.	Eaten or injected.
Heroin (also called dope, junk, scag, horse, smack, and "H")	Made from morphine by chemical process. About seven times stronger than morphine. Used by 90 percent of all narcotics addicts. Not used medically. Against the law except when used in government-approved experiments.	Inhaled or injected.
Methadone (also called dolophine)	Made in laboratories. Does not come from the poppy flower. Often given to people trying to break the heroin habit. Satisfies an addict's desire for heroin, but allows addict to live a more normal life.	Injected or eaten.
Meperidine (also called demerol)	Made in laboratories. Does not come from the poppy flower. Used medically as a pain reliever.	Injected or eaten.

NARCOTICS

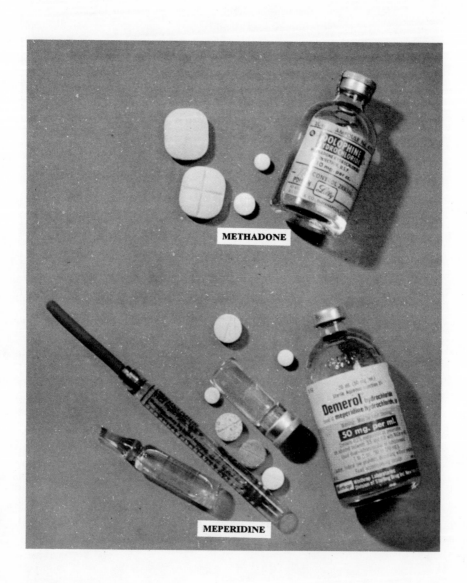

METHADONE

MEPERIDINE

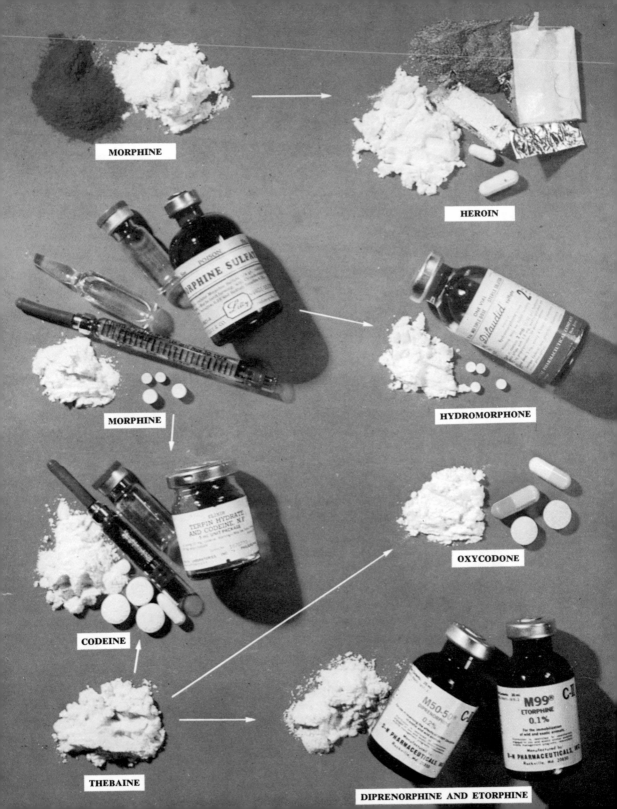

MORPHINE

HEROIN

MORPHINE

HYDROMORPHONE

CODEINE

OXYCODONE

THEBAINE

DIPRENORPHINE AND ETORPHINE

STIMULANTS AND DEPRESSANTS

People in every society, at every period in history, have had problems. Our modern age is no exception. The style of life today is very fast-moving. Many people are finding it hard to keep up and still be comfortable and happy about who they are. It's easy to get thrown off the track.

More and more people seem to be turning to pills for help in smoothing over life's rough spots. Millions of people today have at one time or another taken pills to relax them. Millions more have taken sleeping pills at some time in their lives. Drugs that provide pep to people who feel tired or uninterested in life are also popular. And available statistics include only legal prescriptions obtained from a doctor. Many more people buy these pills illegally and use them for recreational purposes.

Drugs are complex chemicals, and each one has many different effects on the body. In general, however, the group of drugs known as **downers,** or **depressants,** are drugs that slow down, or depress, the body's nervous system. **Uppers,** or **stimulants,** are drugs that have the opposite effect. They stimulate the body's nervous system.

DOWNERS: THE TRANQUILIZERS

One group of downers, the **tranquilizers,** are meant to calm people who are upset. Very strong tranquilizers such as thorazine are used in the treatment of mental illness. Similar kinds are used to treat high blood pressure or to relax muscles that are very tight. Milder tranquilizers such as valium and librium are often prescribed by doctors for people who are nervous and anxious— often enough, in fact, to make these among the most commonly prescribed drugs today.

People who are taking tranquilizers must be careful to stay under a doctor's care. Strong tranquilizers often cause dangerous side effects, and in extremely large doses may even be fatal. Some side effects of thorazine, for example, are drowsiness, dryness of the mouth, nausea, sensitivity to light, and a skin rash. Thorazine can also cause trembling, drooling, yellowing of the skin, a sore throat, and thin blood.

The milder tranquilizers may also have unpleasant side effects. Valium, for example, can cause drowsiness, a stomach upset, a skin rash, and a lack of coordination in some people. Moreover, recent studies have suggested that repeated use of mild tranquilizers may make people less able to cope with changes in their environment.

MORE DOWNERS: THE SEDATIVES

Other downers, called **sedatives,** are meant to put a patient to sleep. **Barbiturates** are the most commonly prescribed sleeping pills. They are also given to relax patients before surgery and as a pain reliever during childbirth.

There are many other sedatives available that are not barbiturates. Quaalude (also sometimes known as mandrax), for example, is one popular type of nonbarbiturate sedative.

Barbiturates are powerful drugs. Side effects that have been reported include depression, listlessness, a skin rash, bad dreams, and difficulty in breathing. Many overdoses occur. Since these drugs dull the mind, users sometimes forget how many pills they have taken. In their confusion, they take too many. An overdose of barbiturates can cause coma and death.

The use of barbiturates over a long period of time may cause addiction. People who are addicted to barbiturates may also be addicted to other drugs that depress the body's nervous system, such as alcohol or narcotics. A person who is withdrawing from barbiturates must be careful to avoid these other drugs, too. BARBITURATE ADDICTION IS ALSO DANGEROUS BECAUSE SUDDEN WITHDRAWAL CAN CAUSE DEATH. Under a doctor's care, the addict gradually cuts down on the dosage taken.

OTHER DANGERS OF DOWNERS

In high doses, downers produce a dreamy, floating feeling. Perhaps because of this, all downers have a tendency to create psychological dependence very quickly. They are popular with people who want to escape from the problems of life.

DEPRESSANTS

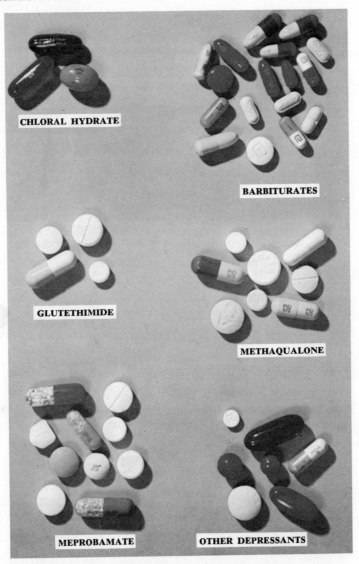

CHLORAL HYDRATE

BARBITURATES

GLUTETHIMIDE

METHAQUALONE

MEPROBAMATE

OTHER DEPRESSANTS

STIMULANTS

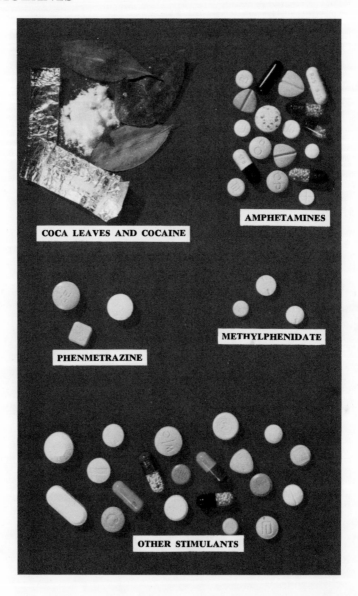

COCA LEAVES AND COCAINE

AMPHETAMINES

PHENMETRAZINE

METHYLPHENIDATE

OTHER STIMULANTS

People on downers should not drive or operate machinery. Their slowed reactions can cause accidents.

Finally, no downer should be taken along with another drug unless a doctor has okayed the combination. Downers react harmfully with many other substances. Mixing barbiturates and alcohol, for example, can cause death.

UPPERS: THE AMPHETAMINES

Speed. Wake-ups. Pep pills. Ups. All these are popular names for a group of drugs called amphetamines. These popular names give a good description of the effects amphetamines have on the body. Amphetamines are stimulants. They excite the nervous system, and increase energy, alertness, and tone in some muscles. A dose of these drugs may cause the lungs to work faster and the blood pressure to rise. A person on amphetamines also feels more excited, more active, and more talkative than usual. The user often displays great confidence, an "I can do anything" attitude.

Amphetamines, when used medically, are taken as a pill or capsule. They are used in the treatment of a rare sleeping disorder called narcolepsy. They are sometimes prescribed for dieters, since short-term use can decrease appetite. Amphetamines are also used for children who are *too* active. These so-called hyperactive children are unable to control themselves. They cannot concentrate and have trouble sitting still. Amphetamines have the reverse effect in these cases. Instead of making the children more excited, the drugs calm them down. Researchers are not sure why. Amphetamines were also once widely prescribed for people who were feeling tired or depressed. However, today they have been replaced by newer drugs called antidepressants.

Another common use of amphetamines is to increase performance, although this is not recognized as an appropriate medical use. People who want to do too much in too short a time sometimes take amphetamines. Students cramming for an exam, for example, might take them to stay awake all night. Amphetamines are also sometimes taken for "kicks." When taken for this purpose, they are often injected into a vein, a method that produces a feeling of great excitement.

Unfortunately, amphetamines have severe side effects. They tend to cause psychological dependence. Some scientists believe they are also physically addictive. Furthermore, the body really can't stand too fast a pace. If you do eight days' work in one, you will be eight times as tired when you are finished.

Some people can't cope with the tiredness and depression that follow amphetamine use. So they take more speed to get high again. The body's tolerance grows rapidly, and a bad pattern is established. More and more speed is taken to get high, followed by deeper and deeper "crashes" at the end. The body and mind begin to show the strain. Long-term use of amphetamines may cause a constant state of tension, high blood pressure, an irregular heartbeat, and a heart attack. Speed freaks, as regular users are called, begin to feel suspicious and irritable all the time. They often lose contact with reality and show symptoms of mental illness. Some commit suicide.

If a speed freak is unable to obtain regular doses of the drug, he or she may suffer severe withdrawal symptoms. These include depression, anxiety, headaches, breathing difficulty, sweating, shivers, and constipation. As users become more involved with the drug, they neglect to eat, rest, or take care of their bodies. They become thin and worn out. Many contract serious illnesses such as pneumonia and hepatitis. Some users die from these diseases. Others die from overdoses of the drugs, which cause convulsions (violent muscle spasms), coma, and death.

COCAINE

Cocaine also speeds up the nervous system, but it is milder than the amphetamines. Cocaine is a white powder that is made from the leaves of the coca bush, which grows in the mountains of South America. As far back as a thousand years ago the Indians of South America chewed coca leaves to give themselves more energy.

Cocaine is occasionally used medically in some operations. The nonmedical use of cocaine is against the law. Still, among some groups it is fashionable to take cocaine for recreation. It is very expensive, so the dealer who sells cocaine usually mixes it with cheaper substances.

Cocaine can be injected or taken by mouth, but it is usually inhaled. When a person takes cocaine, the blood vessels become narrowed. The blood pressure and temperature of the body rise. The heart beats faster, and the pupils of the eyes grow larger. The person feels high. The user is excited and talkative and has a "sitting on top of the world" feeling. Cocaine also temporarily numbs the part of the body it touches.

Repeated use of cocaine can cause psychological dependence and mental confusion. Some scientists believe it also causes physical addiction. If it is inhaled repeatedly, the lining of the nose can become damaged. In severe cases, the partition between the nostrils breaks.

[35

Left: a Bolivian gathering coca leaves.
Right: the coca plant.

COMMON UPPERS AND DOWNERS

Name	Description	How Used
Tranquilizers (including valium, milltown, librium, and equanil)	Calming, but do not usually produce sleep.	Usually eaten.
Barbiturates (including phenobarbital, nembutal, amytal, seconal. Also called reds, blues, barbs, downers, and yellows.)	Sleeping pills. Relieve tension.	Usually eaten.
Amphetamines (including benzedrine, dexedrine, and desoxyn. Also called speed, bennies, dexies, pep pills, and wake-ups.)	Excite the nervous system. Give a feeling of self-confidence and energy.	Eaten or injected.
Cocaine (also called snow)	Excites the nervous system. Gives a feeling of strength and power.	Injected, rubbed in mouth, or inhaled.

DRUGS THAT CHANGE REALITY

From the very first moment of life, we receive information from the world around us. This information comes to us through our senses. It is passed along to the brain by way of nerves. The brain, upon receiving the data, interprets for the mind what the body has sensed.

When a person has a **hallucination,** something may be sensed that does not exist at all in the outside world. The person's mind may experience, say, an object, a person, a place, or a sound that isn't there. Or, the person may see something different from what is really there. A person having this kind of hallucination might see a cat and think it's a lion. Certain drugs are known to be **hallucinogens.** That is, they are substances that can cause a person to hallucinate. Other similar substances do not seem to cause hallucinations. Yet they do change reality in many of the same ways as hallucinogenic drugs.

No one really knows how or why hallucinations occur. We are fairly sure that they involve some malfunction in the nervous system. Information in the brain is transmitted from nerve cell to nerve cell with the help of certain chemicals. Research has shown that some drugs decrease the production of some of these chemicals in the brain. When this happens, the person hallucinates. Exactly why this chemical change causes hallucinations, however, is not understood.

One area of hallucination research involves the unconscious mind. We receive and store much more information in our minds than we realize. Also, we bury some information that may not be pleasant to recall. This information is called unconscious, because we cannot think of it or recall it at will. Thoughts, memories, and attitudes that we can recall easily are called conscious.

Unconscious information is thought to be stored in the right half of the brain. Conscious information is stored in the left. The two halves are connected by a thick bunch of nerves. Some scientists theorize that hallucinations occur when something abnormal happens to the pathway between the right and left brain. The conscious brain may then be flooded with thoughts that are usually stored in the unconscious. Drugs that cause hallucinations may affect this pathway.

Many drugs can cause hallucinations. The drugs discussed in this chapter, however, are often taken for just that purpose. The user means them to change the way he or she experiences reality.

LSD

There are many hallucinogens, including mescaline, psilocybin, and psilocin. Lysergic acid diethylamide (LSD) is probably the most well known. It is so powerful that the tiniest drop taken into the body will have a strong effect on the brain.

When people take LSD (and other hallucinogens), they are said to be "on a trip." And what a strange trip it is! Super-intense images, weird sounds, and fantastic visions are often reported. Many users feel that they gain a completely new view of themselves and the world after taking an "acid" trip. Others describe their trips almost as if they were religious experiences. In fact, many native American Indian tribes have used hallucinogenic drugs as part of their religious celebrations.

An LSD trip usually lasts for a few hours, but "flashbacks" can occur months later. During a flashback, the user suddenly feels as if he or she were "tripping" again, even though no additional dose of the drug was taken. Scientists believe that the reason for this is that these drugs may be stored in the nerve cells of the brain for long periods. Long after the original trip is over, something triggers the release of the stored drug, and the trip begins again. What this trigger may be is not known. In one study, however, researchers found that LSD users who frequently smoked marijuana were more likely to "flashback" than other users.

Unfortunately, LSD sessions are not always pleasant. Without warning they can turn into "bad" trips. During these times, the drug user feels frightened, suspicious, or out of control. No one really understands why some trips are mostly pleasant and others turn into nightmares. One possible reason is that whatever is deep inside a person's mind is brought out by the drug. If the user has been burying feelings of fright, great fear may surface during a trip. Another person, or the same person in a different mood, may have a happier experience. All the hallucinogens seem to have this double personality.

Trips may also be different because the drugs are not always the same in strength and purity. Since hallucinogens are against

HALLUCINOGENS

PCP

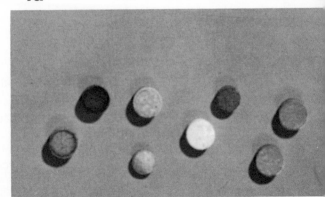

LSD

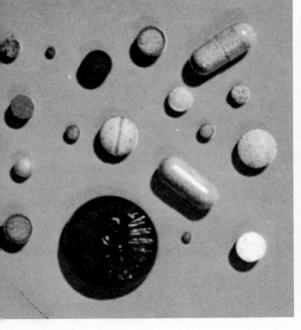

MDA

the law, they are usually bought from dealers on the street. There are no government regulations to protect the buyer. What the seller calls LSD may not really be LSD. In fact, LSD is very often mixed with cheaper drugs and sold as pure. Nor is there any way to tell how strong a certain batch of a drug is.

There are other dangers. Because people taking LSD are not able to think rationally, they sometimes do strange things. A number of users have been killed from having fallen out of a window. Others have been blinded because they stared too long at the sun.

Scientists do not fully understand the effects of LSD and other hallucinogens on the body. A recent study, however, showed that rats who were given LSD had a higher than usual percentage of offspring with birth defects. At present, LSD is not approved for general medical use. Some doctors are using LSD experimentally in the treatment of alcoholics and the mentally ill. All other uses are against the law.

PCP ("ANGEL DUST")

PCP is a relative newcomer to the drug scene. It was developed in the 1950s to make people sleep during operations. However, doctors who administered it soon noticed that it often caused their patients to experience anxiety, confusion, hallucinations, or seizures. So it was quickly dropped from the approved list of drugs for human beings. Today the drug is still sometimes used medically as a tranquilizer for large animals such as lions and elephants. And, although it is illegal for all other uses, many people use angel dust to get high. In fact, a recent survey showed that millions of people have used angel dust at least once, and use among teen-agers has grown at an alarming rate.

The scientific name of this drug is phencyclidine hydrochloride, PCP for short. It is a white powder that can be easily made in a laboratory. Since PCP is cheap, pushers often substitute it for more expensive drugs, marketing it as LSD or heroin. PCP users take the drug in the form of small pills or spray it on marijuana or tobacco and smoke it. As with LSD, the effects of PCP are very unpredictable. A user can smoke it any number of times and feel only a pleasant high. Then suddenly, without warning, a PCP trip can turn into a disaster. Sometimes a person's very first experience with the drug can be bad.

Many PCP users feel tremendous anger while under the influence of the drug. They may do violence to themselves or to others. Authorities say that PCP use has resulted in a significant number of murders and suicides. Some PCP users don't become violent but go completely out of control. The effects of a bad PCP reaction can last up to a month. In severe cases, the user has convulsions, goes into a coma, and dies. Since PCP users often feel confused, they get into many unusual accidents. Several PCP users who were swimming, for example, drowned though they were only in shallow water. One user drowned while taking a shower.

SNIFFING

Other popular drugs are chemicals most people don't think of as drugs—cleaning fluids, some glues, some aerosol sprays, and gasoline (petrol). These substances have very strong smells caused by the liquid in them slowly changing into a gas and escaping into the air. When you breathe in this gas, the drugs contained in it are inhaled into your body.

MARIJUANA WITH "JOINTS"

HASHISH

If you are using any of these products, removing a stain with cleaning fluid for example, you can't help inhaling some of the fumes. That small amount won't have any noticeable effect on you. But some people "sniff" these products deliberately, in order to get high. People who do this take in a large amount of the chemical by inhaling deeply. Sometimes they fill a bag with the chemical and breathe into it in order to get a higher concentration of the fumes.

Sniffing these gases causes a drunk, dizzy feeling. Hues seem brighter, and the user feels reckless and all-powerful. Some people hallucinate. But like all other drugs that change reality, sniffing chemicals can cause bad reactions. Headaches, memory loss, lack of coordination, and panic are some of the symptoms that can occur. Because users become mentally confused while under the drug's influence, many have accidents they wouldn't otherwise have had. One boy walked off a roof after sniffing glue. Sniffing also has harmful effects on the body. Liver, kidney, bone marrow, and brain damage can result from inhaling these chemicals.

MARIJUANA

Marijuana is the name given to the dried leaves of the hemp plant. These leaves can be cooked into food and eaten, but they are usually smoked. In a few places the medical use of marijuana is legal. In these places, marijuana is a prescription drug and is used in the treatment of the eye disease glaucoma. It may also be used to relieve the nausea experienced by people who are taking anticancer drugs. The use of marijuana for recreation is against the law everywhere. Nevertheless, it is one of the most popular recreational drugs around today. Millions of people are regular users.

Most people who smoke marijuana say it makes them feel pleasantly relaxed. Hues and sounds seem more intense. Often, the user's sense of time and space changes. A minute may seem like an hour. Giddiness and some mental confusion are common. Since there is also usually some loss of coordination, a person's driving skills are affected. Many people report an increase in appetite and thirst. Marijuana also increases the heart rate, reduces pressure inside the eyeball, and irritates blood vessels behind the eye.

As with all the other drugs discussed in this chapter, marijuana sometimes causes unpleasant reactions. Some people experience irritability, nervousness, or anxiety. However, hallucinations are extremely rare. This may be because the marijuana sold in the West is often very mild. In India, where more powerful forms of the drug are used, there are more frequent reports of hallucinations.

Marijuana may cause psychological dependence, but it is not physically addictive. Is it safe for repeated use? At the present time, no one really knows. Only a few carefully controlled long-term studies have been done, but even these have yielded conflicting results.

One type of marijuana that is almost certainly dangerous is marijuana that has been sprayed with paraquat. Paraquat is a chemical that is used to kill weeds. Some marijuana grown in Mexico has been sprayed with this chemical. If you smoke marijuana coated with this substance, you will probably take some of the paraquat into your lungs. Most doctors agree that this is harmful. Unfortunately, you can't tell just by looking at it if a batch of marijuana has paraquat on it. A laboratory test is necessary.

DRUGS THAT CHANGE REALITY

Name	Description	How Used
LSD (also called acid)	Causes hallucinations.	Usually eaten.
PCP (also called angel dust, killer weed, hog, wobble, magic mist, tic tac, superweed, and superjoint)	Animal tranquilizer used by people to get high.	Sniffed, smoked, chewed, or injected.
Chemicals that may be sniffed (including acetone, naphtha, carbon tetrachloride, and toluene)	When inhaled produce feelings of drunkenness, dizziness, well-being. Everything seems bright; users feel all-powerful.	Inhaled.
Marijuana (also called pot, smoke, grass, weed, dope, reefers, joints; concentrated form is called hashish)	Dried leaves from hemp plant. Can produce pleasant high; may cause irritability and nervousness. May make environment seem more beautiful.	Eaten or smoked.

TOBACCO
AND
ALCOHOL

To most people, taking a drug means swallowing a pill or receiving an injection. But a person smoking a cigarette or drinking a cocktail is taking a drug, too. Tobacco smoke contains many drugs, including nicotine and tar. Beer, wine, and liquor, on the other hand, contain only one drug. But that drug, alcohol, has a tremendous effect on the human body.

No prescription is needed to buy these drugs, and they are sold just about everywhere. But though they are easy to get hold of, they are far from harmless. Each deserves a closer look.

TOBACCO

The tobacco that is smoked is made from the dried leaves of the tobacco plant. This plant once grew wild all over the Western Hemisphere. It was first smoked by the ancient Maya Indians of Central America. When Europeans began to explore the Americas, they tried smoking tobacco, too, and brought it home with them. In our own century, the habit of smoking tobacco has spread to every corner of the world. It has become big business, with millions spent each year on cigarettes, cigars, and pipe tobacco.

What Smoking Does to Your Body

When smokers inhale the smoke from their cigarettes, they take the drugs contained in the tobacco into their bodies. Only three seconds after the first puff, nicotine makes the blood vessels become narrower. The blood pressure rises, and the heart has to work harder to circulate the blood through the body. Carbon monoxide, a poisonous gas in the tobacco smoke, begins to replace some of the oxygen in the blood. The smoker has to breathe faster in order to take in enough oxygen. Tar and other irritating substances are deposited on the lungs.

Beginning smokers may feel the effects of the drugs in tobacco on their bodies. They may cough and feel dizzy or nauseous. Their skin may feel cold and sweaty, and they may have diarrhea. But as people continue to smoke, their bodies build up tolerance to the drugs. They no longer *feel* sick after smoking a cigarette.

Unfortunately, the fact that an experienced smoker doesn't feel sick doesn't mean no harm is being done to the body. Studies have shown that a habit of smoking even a half a pack of an average brand of cigarettes a day can be hazardous to health. And the damage increases as more cigarettes are smoked. Moreover, the effects add up over the years. Someone who has been smoking for ten years, for example, will have more health problems than someone who has smoked for only five years.

By the time a heavy smoker reaches middle age, the heart and blood vessels begin to feel the strain. The smoker's lungs are covered with tar and other chemicals. All the parts of the body that the smoke touches have been irritated. The results of all this have been clearly documented. When a middle-aged heavy smoker and nonsmoker are compared, the smoker is 70 to 300 times more likely to have heart disease. A male smoker is 50 percent more likely to suffer a stroke, a life-threatening condition in which the flow of blood to the brain is blocked. If the smoker is a woman, she is 100 percent more likely to have a stroke. And a woman smoker who takes birth control pills (pills that prevent pregnancy) is ten times more likely to die of a heart attack than a woman who uses neither birth control pills nor tobacco.

Smokers of either sex are eleven times more likely to die of lung cancer. Lung cancer is a serious disease in which there is abnormal growth of cells in the lungs. It is often fatal. Smokers also have increased risk of cancers of the larynx, esophagus, bladder, and kidneys, and other diseases of the lungs such as emphysema and bronchitis.

All these statistics add up to this: where smoking is prevalent, someone dies every minute and a half from its effects. A two-pack-a-day smoker will probably shorten his or her life by 8.3 years. To put it yet another way, every cigarette a heavy smoker smokes shortens that smoker's life by six minutes!

With odds like these, it seems crazy for people to continue smoking. Yet people do. Psychological dependence on tobacco develops easily and is hard to overcome. Some scientists also believe that nicotine is physically addictive.

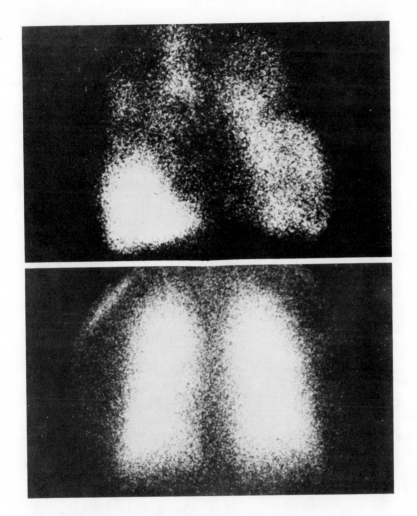

This krypton lung scan shows the difference between the lungs of someone with emphysema (top) and the lungs of a healthy person. The dark spots are areas blocked by the disease.

A shopper buying alcohol.

ALCOHOL

Ask any person what drug causes the most problems. Chances are the answer will be heroin, LSD, or another drug that is against the law. But surprisingly enough, the most misused drug today is alcohol. Consider these facts: recent studies show that 40 percent of all arrests in the United States are related to drinking. In half of all the car accidents where someone died, one or more of the drivers had been drinking. One-half of all murders, and one-third of all suicides are alcohol-related.

In spite of this, alcohol is not a totally unsafe drug. For the majority of people, having a drink is a pleasant, relaxing experience. What makes for the difference between the use and abuse of alcohol?

What Alcohol Does to Your Body
The alcohol found in drinks is called ethyl, or grain, alcohol. Other types of alcohol, such as the alcohol used in rubdowns, are poisonous to drink. All alcoholic drinks contain the same alcohol, but in differing amounts. That is why whiskey and other hard liquors are stronger than beer or wine. They contain more alcohol. This doesn't mean, however, that people who drink beer or wine can't get drunk. They simply have to drink more of it to get the same amount of alcohol in their bodies.

After the alcohol enters the body, it passes into the stomach. Some of it is absorbed into the bloodstream from there. The rest is absorbed in the small intestine. Once in the bloodstream, alcohol circulates to all parts of the body. The liver begins to break down the alcohol into other substances. The liver can process about 1/3 of an ounce (10 ml) of alcohol an hour. If more than that amount is taken in, the alcohol builds up in the blood, and the person becomes drunk.

Alcohol acts on the brain and nervous system. The effects of the drug depend mostly on how much alcohol is in the blood. If the amount is small, the person feels happy, warm, and relaxed. As the concentration of alcohol in the blood builds up, the person becomes less coordinated. The hands may shake, and memory and alertness are decreased. The part of the brain that gives one a sense of self-control is affected. Thus, drinkers sometimes do things that would be embarrassing to them if they were sober. Some people argue or fight, others just act silly. If more alcohol is drunk, the drinker's ability to walk and talk properly will be affected. At this point, continued drinking could cause unconsciousness or even death.

As the effects of a drunken spell wear off, the drinker feels "hung over." Some symptoms of a hangover are an upset stomach, unusual thirst, and a headache.

Alcoholism
Excessive drinking over a long period of time can cause serious problems. It can damage a person's health, ruin personal relationships, and interfere with school or work. When the urge to drink becomes uncontrollable, the drinker is said to be suffering from alcoholism.

An alcoholic is psychologically dependent on and physically addicted to alcohol. As with any other addiction, an alcoholic will experience withdrawal symptoms if a dose of the drug is missed. These include anxiety, trembling, diarrhea, nausea, weakness, and convulsions. Some alcoholics hallucinate during withdrawal and lose contact with reality. Such hallucinations are called delirium tremens (DTs). Withdrawing from alcohol is difficult and dangerous. It is important for an alcoholic to have medical supervision during withdrawal. Without a doctor's help, the alcoholic may die.

If it is not treated, alcoholism results in great tragedy. Alcoholics shorten their life span by an average of ten to twelve years. They suffer liver and brain damage and have a greater than normal chance of heart disease and cancer. Since drinking also causes a lack of coordination and judgment, alcoholics often injure themselves and others in accidents they cause.

But physical damage is only part of the problem. The drug becomes the alcoholic's whole life. Everything else—work, family, friends—becomes unimportant.

Few alcoholics (less than 6 percent) are permanently cured, but the disease can be controlled. If you know someone with a drinking problem, by all means urge him or her to seek help. Over 50 percent of all those who come in for treatment succeed in conquering alcoholism, at least for a time. One of the best treatments available is through an organization called Alcoholics Anonymous (AA). AA is composed of ex-addicts who help each other stay away from drinking "one day at a time." Many hospitals, businesses, and the armed forces also offer treatment for alcoholics.

WHAT WILL YOU DO?

Each day you make decisions that shape your life—what to wear, what to eat, what to study in school, whom to choose as a friend. Each individual decision seems unimportant. But through the years your choices add up and help make you the special person you are.

Decisions about taking drugs will have to be made again and again, in different ways. Should I take aspirin for this headache? Should I go drinking with my friends? Smoke marijuana at the party? Try LSD, cocaine, or heroin?

No one can make these decisions for you. If you really want to take a drug, you will. Even if your parents, your school, and the laws of your country say you should not.

But drugs are powerful, and decisions about them should not be made lightly. Before you swallow, puff, or sniff, THINK! What is this drug? What will it do to my body? What will it do to my mind? If the drug is against the law, am I willing to risk being arrested? If the drug is habit-forming, am I willing to take it for the rest of my life?

We are all born with a desire for new experiences. You can see this easily if you watch a baby exploring. The baby wants to see, hear, taste, and touch everything. There is nothing wrong with curiosity. It is natural and good.

But as we grow older, we learn to think beforehand of the results of our actions. If allowed to, a baby will crawl into a fireplace, just to see what the flames are like. A more mature person may have the same curiosity. But knowing the probable results of crawling into the fire is enough to stop him or her. If you think about what you are doing beforehand, you may decide that satisfying your curiosity about a particular drug is just not worth the risk.

Another basic human need is to escape. Life can be hard, and everybody needs to run away from their problems sometimes. But people who run away all the time only end up running into a new set of problems. Moreover, they never develop problem-solving skills. They never take control of themselves and of their lives.

If you are unhappy with your life or find you need some way to escape once in a while, you should consider some choices other than drugs that are open to you. Meditation, yoga, and even daydreaming can change the way you experience reality. Talking over your problems with a trusted friend or relative might make them easier to solve. And if these methods don't help, there are professionals specially trained and available to you.

Drugs, by themselves, are only tools. They are not right or wrong. Used intelligently, drugs can save and enrich lives. Used improperly, they can take over lives, or even end them. What role will drugs play in *your* life? The decision, in the end, is yours.

GLOSSARY OF IMPORTANT TERMS

Note: Most individual drugs are not listed in this glossary. Information on them in the text may be found by using the index at the end of the book.

Addiction: A drug habit in which the user cannot stop taking the drug without experiencing withdrawal symptoms. Can be physical or psychological or both. A person with a drug addiction also develops tolerance.

Alcohol: A drug found in wine, beer, and hard liquor. Addiction to alcohol is called alcoholism.

Amphetamines: Drugs that excite the nervous system.

Antibiotics: Drugs that kill or weaken certain bacteria germs.

Barbiturates: Drugs that calm people and make them sleep.

Caffeine: A drug found in coffee, tea, and cola drinks. Not proven to be harmful in moderate amounts.

Depressants: See **Downers.**

Dosage: The amount of a drug that is taken.

Downers: Drugs that slow down, or depress, the body's nervous system.

Drugs: Chemicals that when taken into the body alter normal bodily processes.

Hallucination: Seeing something that isn't there or seeing something different from what is there.

Hallucinogen: A drug that causes hallucinations.

Medicine: A drug that fights disease and restores the bodily processes to normal or a drug that eliminates the symptoms of a disease, though not the disease itself.

Narcotics: A group of drugs that are highly addictive and relieve pain. Most are made from the poppy flower, but some are produced in laboratories.

Over-the-counter (OTC) drugs: Drugs that can be bought by anyone.

Prescription drugs: Drugs that can be bought only if the buyer has a written order—a prescription—from a doctor.

Sedatives: Downers, meant to calm or put a person to sleep.

Side effect: An effect a drug has on the body that is not intended; in most cases the side effect is not beneficial.

Stimulants: See **Uppers.**

Tobacco: A leaf that contains a number of drugs; is usually smoked. Tobacco is psychologically addictive and may be physically addictive also.

Tolerance: A condition in which more and more of the drug is needed to produce the desired effect.

Tranquilizers: Downers that calm people.

Uppers: Drugs that excite, or stimulate, the nervous system.

Withdrawal symptoms: Physical and psychological symptoms experienced when an addict stops taking the drug he or she is addicted to.

IF YOU
NEED HELP

Many communities have hot lines or drop-in treatment facilities for people who need help with a drug problem. Most of these places can also help you get further information.

The following organizations have branches in several areas. The location of the chapter nearest you may be obtained by writing to the national headquarters or looking in a local telephone directory.

Synanon Foundation, Inc.
(for help with a variety of drugs)
18500 State Route 1
Marshall, California 94940 ■ 415-663-8111

Rubicon, Inc.
(for help with a variety of drugs)
1208 West Franklin Street
Richmond, Virginia 23220 ■ 804-359-3255

Odyssey House
(for help with a variety of drugs)
c/o Odyssey Institute
309–311 East Sixth Street
New York, New York 10003 ■ 212-741-9597

Pills Anonymous
(for help with addiction to uppers and downers.
There are only a few chapters at this time,
but many more are being formed.)
205 West End Avenue
New York, New York 10023 ■ 212-874-0700

General Services Board of Alcoholics Anonymous
468 Park Avenue South
New York, New York 10016 ■ 212-686-1100

Al-Anon
(for relatives of those with a drinking problem)
1 Park Avenue
New York, New York 10010 ■ 212-481-6565

Release is a British organization (1, Elgin Avenue, London W9 3PR) that provides help and information for any drug-related problem. **Cure** (533a, Kings Road, London SW10) also offers help to addicts in Britain. For help in coping with a drinking problem in Britain, contact **Alcoholics Anonymous** at 11, Redcliffe Gardens, London SW10.

Smokenders is a commercial organization that attempts to help people quit smoking. Chapters are located in many places. For the one nearest you, look in your local telephone directory.

Tips on quitting may also be obtained by writing to your local chapter of the **American Cancer Society.**

BOOKS FOR FURTHER READING

Donahue, Parnell, and Capellaro, Helen.
Germs Make Me Sick.
New York: Alfred A. Knopf, 1975.

Evans, Roberta.
Alcohol and Alcoholism.
New York: Franklin Watts, 1976.

Gorodetzky, Charles, and Christian, Samuel T.
What You Should Know About Drugs.
New York: Harcourt Brace Jovanovich, 1970.

Marr, John S.
The Good Drug and the Bad Drug.
New York: M. Evans & Co., 1970.

Navarra, John Gabriel.
Drugs and Man.
Garden City, N.Y.: Doubleday & Co., 1973.

Sonnett, Sherry.
Smoking.
New York: Franklin Watts, 1977.

INDEX

ABOUT THE AUTHOR

Presently a writer by profession, Geraldine Woods taught grades five through eight in a New York City school for several years. For Franklin Watts she has authored *Saudi Arabia,* another in the First Book series. Geraldine, her husband, and their young son make their home in New York City.